CW01011326

A DEFINITION OF WHITE PRIVILEGE

Jodie M. Williams

*With Love
Joelie
X*

Copyright © 2020 by J. M. Williams

All rights reserved. No part of this book may be reproduced or used in any manner without written permission of the copyright owner except for the use of quotations in a book review.

FIRST EDITION

Published by J. M. Williams
ISBN: 978-1-8381179-0-0

For more information, address: Jodie.M.Williams@hotmail.co.uk

To all the people who helped this work come together, to those who contributed, to those who continue to fight daily for equality, for a more inclusive world - Thank You.

Growing up I always knew I was different to many people around me. I was raised in a white family, with white parents but I was a Black child. Mixed race to be specific, however to the world I was Black. From a young age, I knew there were very subtle differences in how the world treated people like me and sometimes, not so subtle.

As I grew, I learned to navigate through these, what I have come to know as microaggressions, nuanced behaviours and differences.

I have, and will always see my differences as a positive, something to be acknowledged, celebrated, loved.

We live in a world in which the default settings centre whiteness. White privilege, has at times been rather difficult to explain, sometimes part of living with it, means you have no idea you have it, however those affected by it can usually provide many examples as to how it impacts their day to day lives.

During June 2020, I started to document my experiences of white privilege and also asked people about their lived experiences of white privilege. I asked them to provide examples of how it affected their day to day lives, in addition to sharing mine. The feedback was phenomenal and it was very easy to see that this is a collective experience shared by many of us, who aren't part of the worlds 'default settings'.
These lived examples were then curated in an online exhibition at www.boujiemedia.co.uk

To people reading this with shared experiences, you are not alone, and to people reading who don't understand the concept of white privilege, please read with an open mind and understand that these are many people's lived experiences.

White privilege is naturally being able to learn about your history, instead of having it confined to one month in the year.

Where your history is part of the curriculum, where you don't have to sign a petition to have your history taught in schools. My history is referred to as Black history, whereas white history is just called history.

White privilege is being able to watch the TV and see people who look like you and experience stories which are written by people from the same race. Instead I see actors who are typecast and told that it isn't possible to have 2 or 3 Black leads in a TV series because then it becomes niche.

White privilege is not being 5 times more likely to die in childbirth in the NHS.

White privilege is having people from the same race control the media narrative, so that you are represented in every role imaginable.

White privilege is having white actors play Black characters and it not be an issue. But hints at a Black Ariel, Black Annie or Bond is a worldwide issue.

White privilege is having your trauma acknowledged instead of being told 'just get over it' 'it was years ago' 'you have a chip on your shoulder'.

White privilege is not being constantly asked to discuss racism at work, whilst also being censored for your views on racism, because you are the only Black person in your workplace.

White privilege is not being made aware of your colour constantly.

White privilege is not having your hair be an issue in the workplace when you have a new style.

White privilege is being able to buy your child a doll which looks like them and not having to email the store, pay more or wait until they get more diverse dolls.

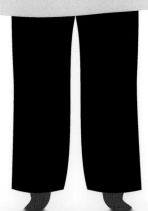

BLACK LIVES MATTER

White privilege is being able to find children's books with a variety of stories about children of the same race.

BLACK LIVES MATTER

White privilege is not being told to go back to the country you came from, when you are British.

White privilege is being able to read a generic news story which is about people of the same race and not have to see ignorant remarks about your own race in the comments section.

White privilege is not having to have conversations about colourism.

White privilege is being able to send your child to school knowing they won't be marked down because the teacher has unchecked unconscious biases and unconscious racist attitudes.

White privilege is never having to hear, you are pretty for a dark skinned woman.

White privilege is never having to have the texture of your hair criminalised and called unprofessional.

White privilege is not having to fight for your child to be in the appropriate class for their grade, even though they are smart enough for it but the teacher can't see past your child's skin colour, and the school continue to refuse to invest in unconscious bias training.

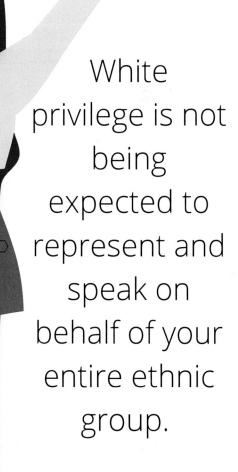

White privilege is not being expected to represent and speak on behalf of your entire ethnic group.

White privilege is being able to say 'I don't see colour' when as a Black person we have been made aware of our colour since we were children, usually by white people.

White privilege is not being more likely to die in the middle of a pandemic from Covid 19 because you take up essential jobs, but don't get the best health care.

White privilege is being able to assume that the racial inequality doesn't exist because it doesn't affect you.

White privilege is seeing yourself represented at board level, as a CEO in FTSE 100 companies, but as a Black woman you aren't given the same representation.

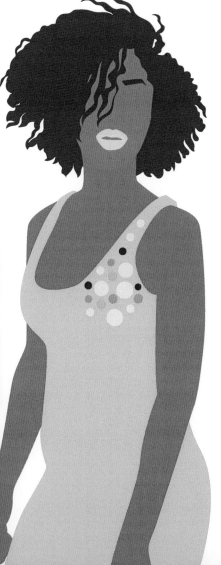

White privilege is then thinking that Black women aren't there because 'it's the best person for the job, and they simply can't be good enough' rather than understanding the actual barriers around bias in the workplace.

White
privilege is
not having to
understand
how Black
people's
natural hair
is perceived.

White privilege is going to a hotel and the shampoo and conditioner is for European straight hair, because that hair is the default, not for Afro hair.

White privilege is not
having to google how racist
a holiday destination is
before you go there.

White privilege is being able to avoid the #travellingwhileblack conversation (check the hashtag on twitter)

White privilege is not understanding the history of colonisation and how it affects us now, and being able to speak positively about Christopher Columbus.

White privilege is being able to buy your shampoo in large supermarkets, but they don't sell shampoo or conditioner for Afro hair.

White privilege is having your hair defined as 'normal' on a shampoo bottle.

White privilege is being able to go to a large well known supermarket and buy 'skin colour' tights and they are for your skin, and if you have Black skin you have to go online to a specialist store. Or wear 'skin colour' tights which aren't a match.

White privilege is being able to easily buy your skin tone in makeup, way before Fenty was a thing.

White privilege is being able to book in a 'photoshoot' pamper day and automatically assume they know how to do your hair and match your skin tone.

White privilege is having your hair type as an emoji by default.

White privilege is never being indirectly asked to explain where your skin colour comes from.

Usually formed in the question of 'where are you from, from'?

White privilege is being able to avoid racially charged microaggressions in the workplace.

White privilege is not being overlooked for promotion due to your skin colour.

McGregor Smith review shows Black, Asian and PoC are more likely to be over looked for promotion than their white counterparts.

White privilege is seeing yourself in magazines and on billboards.

White privilege is going to a job interview and having everyone on the panel have the same skin colour.

White
privilege is
being able
to buy
'nude'
plasters and
they are
your skin
tone.

White privilege is not constantly
having people ask if they can
touch your hair at best, at worst
not even asking.

White privilege is being accepted into the LGBTQ community with open arms, going to pride and getting into bars with ease.

White privilege is not being 7 times more likely to be affected by mental health conditions.

White privilege is not being 4 times more likely to be detained for having a mental health condition, rather than receiving the other forms of support and treatment .

White privilege is being less likely to be at risk of suicide than Black and Asian people and other PoC.

White privilege is being more likely (statistically speaking) to get access to treatment for mental health conditions.

White privilege is going on a night out and not being worried that you won't get in because of the colour of your skin.

White privilege is being able to go shopping and not have security tags on your hair products, or have your products locked behind the counter.

White privilege is being able to go shopping and being less likely (statistically speaking) to be wrongly stopped for shoplifting.

White privilege is not receiving racial abuse in public spaces.

White privilege is not having to worry that you or a family member will suddenly be told one day by the government that you are going to be deported.

White privilege is not having to worry that giving your opinion will render you the 'angry Black person'.

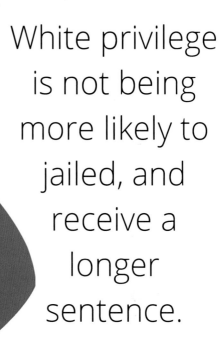

White privilege is not being more likely to jailed, and receive a longer sentence.

*Centre for Justice Innovation report, the Lammy investigation and the sentencing council shows 'Black and minority ethnic offenders are far more likely to be sent to prison'.

White privilege is having your ancestors acknowledged for their efforts in the wars.

White privilege is not having to see statues of slave owners up around the country who murdered and tortured your ancestors for centuries.

White privilege is not being blamed for, and being subject to racial abuse for a virus.

White privilege
is being able
to eat an
avocado whilst
pregnant
without being
hated by the
media.

White privilege is being easily able to buy a birthday card with someone who has the same skin colour.

White privilege is being able to be more annoyed or offended at being called racist that the actual racism, or the comment or action that happened to warrant being called racist.

White privilege is not being considered a risk when it comes to commissioning a programme because people might not watch.

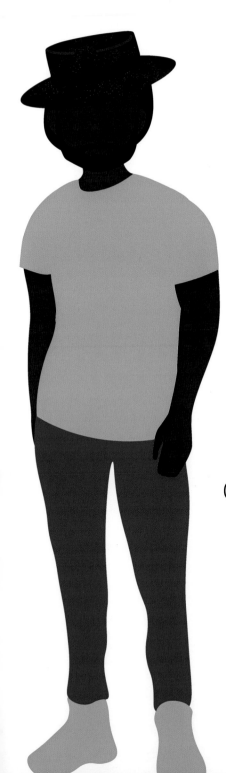

White privilege is being listened to and heard when talking about personal experiences of race and not being told 'they didn't mean it like that' regarding a racially charged comment.

White privilege is not having to prove you are a British Citizen after living and working in the country for almost 60 years.

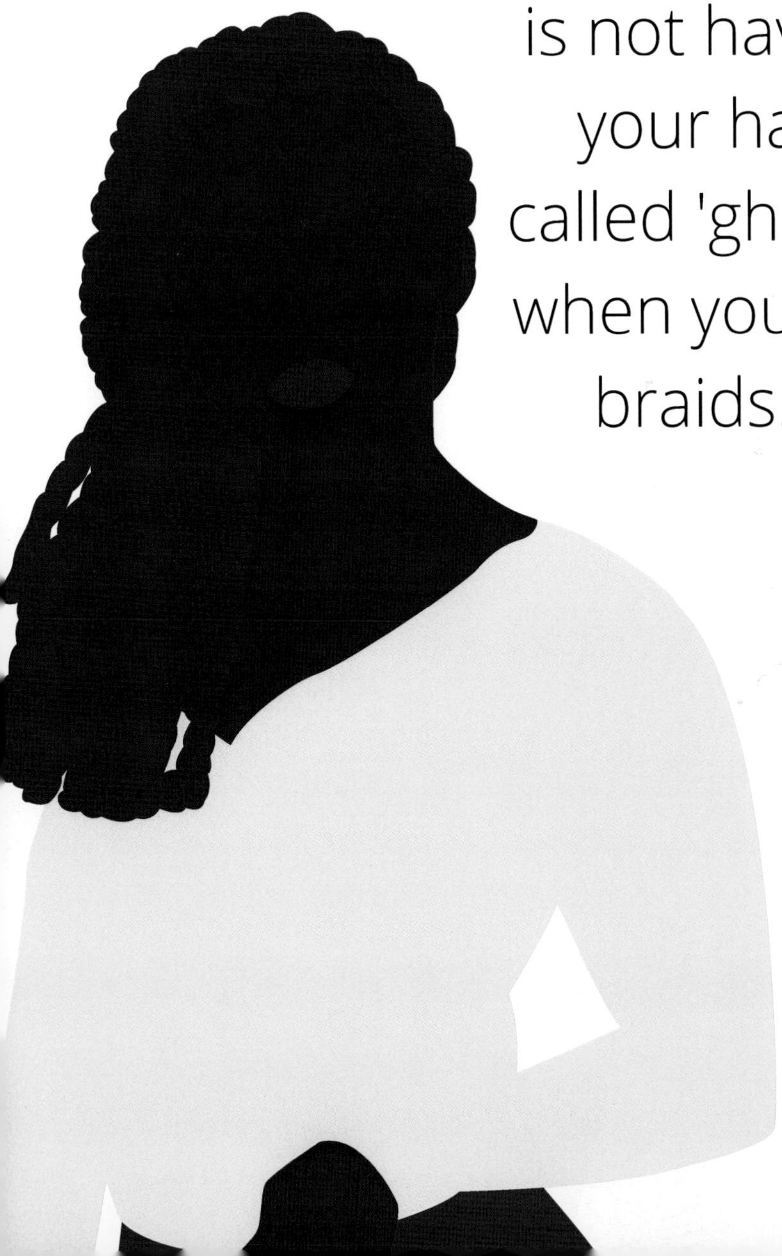

White privilege
is not having
your hair
called 'ghetto'
when you get
braids.

White privilege is being able to use social media without the fear of seeing the police murdering someone because they look like you.

White privilege
is not having
people
constantly call
you ~~the only~~ one of the
other Black
persons name
in the office.

White privilege is getting a job, and being congratulated, not told that you got it to fill the ethnic diversity quota.

White privilege is having your history celebrated, not erased.

White privilege is not having people cross the road, clutch their bags, or lock their car doors when you walk near them.

White privilege is not having to have conversations about race with your young children because of how it is impacting their life.

White privilege is being able to attend a diversity event and not have to be affected by people who say very racist statements, whilst maintaining 'they aren't racist'.

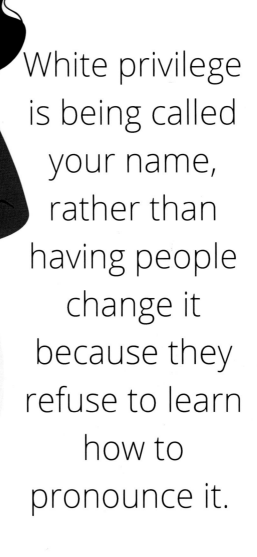

White privilege is being called your name, rather than having people change it because they refuse to learn how to pronounce it.

White privilege is having your skin tone over represented in stock images.

White privilege is being able to move house without having to check how racist an area is.

White privilege is being able to travel in 1st class, without someone assuming you shouldn't be there, based purely on your race

White privilege is being able to visit most high street salons and know they will be able to confidently cater to your hair type.

White privilege is being able to find your food from most large supermarkets, and not having this confined to a 'world food' or an 'ethnic food' section, when all food is 'world food'.

White privilege is being able to speak at an event without people being shocked that 'you speak so well'.

White privilege is being able to speak freely on the phone, and not having to hear 'You don't sound Black' when you meet the person.

White privilege is being able to internet search 'beauty' images and have people from the same race make up the majority of the images.

White privilege is being able to be totally oblivious to the dire state of racism in its present form.

White privilege is being able to use your name on a job application, and know it won't stop you from getting a job.

White privilege is
being able to
accept a new
role and not
have to wonder
if there will be
other people
there of the
same race.

White privilege is avoiding being affected by the UK's ethnicty pay gap.

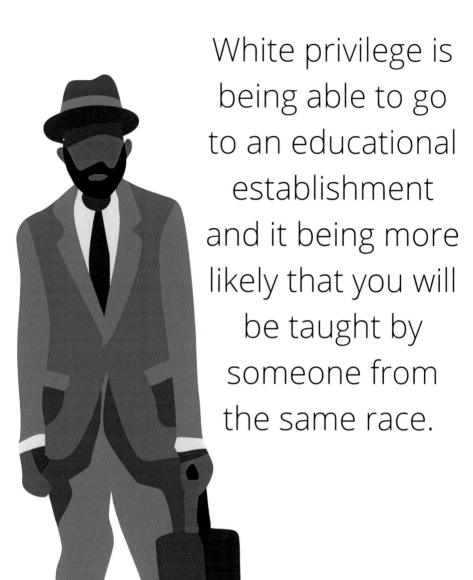

White privilege is being able to go to an educational establishment and it being more likely that you will be taught by someone from the same race.

White privilege is going to the pub quiz with your friends and all the questions are geared towards your lived experiences, heritage and history.

White privilege is being described as 'the person with the blue top' when someone is trying to point you out, rather than 'the Black one'

Thank you for taking the time to read through and to look at other perspectives. This book is filled with many people's experiences of white privilege, and there are many more. To all the contributors, thank you for sharing your lived experiences. We are all different, we are all unique individuals and there is so much beauty and strength in our differences.

To everyone who made this possible, thank you. Special thanks to Boujie Media, who hosted the online exhibition on their website.

"In a racist society it is not enough to be non-racist, we must be anti-racist".

— Angela Y. Davis